The Night We Were Dylan Thomas

Mara Bergman [signature]

MARA BERGMAN

The Night We Were Dylan Thomas

To my dear cousin
+ friend Judith,
who was there
in the beginning
& who I love
being a part of
my life
now,
with much
love,
Mara
xxx

June 2021

PUBLICATIONS
2021

Published by Arc Publications,
Nanholme Mill, Shaw Wood Road
Todmorden OL14 6DA, UK
www.arcpublications.co.uk

978 1910345 51 1 (pbk)
978 1910345 55 9 (ebk)

Design by Tony Ward
Printed in Great Britain by TJ Books, Padstow, Cornwall

Cover illustration by Marcus Ward
reproduced by kind permission of the artist

Supported using public funding by
ARTS COUNCIL ENGLAND
LOTTERY FUNDED

Arc Publications UK and Ireland Series:
Series Editor: Tony Ward

*For Martin
and for my sister, Terri,
and for our mother,
Esta Regent
(1924-2019)*

CONTENTS

IN THE BEGINNING

after Diane Arbus

While the human pincushion was sticking needles through
    his chest
in New Jersey, and contortionist Lydia Suarez
was preparing for an audience in New York City, when
for a penny the mood meter at Coney Island could determine
whether someone was frigid or ardent, tender or harmless, and
Miss Marian Seymour danced with Baron Theo von Roth
at the Grand Opera Ball, my sister and I were growing up
in a world of our own in Wantagh, Long Island, our house
built on the land of a potato farm. In the early years our cousins
pierced layers of ice and lowered strings with hooks.

Only miles away, in Hempstead, female impersonators
may have been smoothing their stockings, applying lipstick
and rouge in a changing room with tattered curtains,
and a beloved dog named Killer may have been buried in
    the cemetery
at Bide-a-Wee, where, years later, my sister would visit the
    homeless dogs
every afternoon, in that summer of 1962 our father's
heart gave up for good. Back at school in September, we spent
weekends at our cousins' and at the end of the year, in Levittown,
someone we didn't know would put up a Christmas tree
in the corner of their living room, next to a sofa covered in plastic.
The clock on top of the TV will say 12.47 forever, the second hand
frozen on 8, the light through the kitchen window a persistent
    muted grey.

HITCH-HIKING ON WANTAGH PARKWAY

for Lori Moses Bennett

With our good legs and cut-offs, the halter tops
    we thought made us older, there was never a doubt
about getting a lift on that particular stretch
    heading south, or that we would reach
the endless sand, hot and gold, the cool Atlantic.
    We'd get rides with a couple of guys
who'd just got their licenses, or sometimes
    a car was so full we could barely squeeze in.
Once, after we'd set off with a middle-aged driver,
    he casually mentioned he might not be going
our way. I don't know about you
    but I never much thought of the danger,
of taking our lives in our hands, entrusting them
    to another. After all, we knew that short run
to Jones Beach like the back of our hands,
    I'd worked the concessions, Field 4, frying burgers.
Remember that time two guys followed us
    onto the sand, shared our blanket, and one of them
admired the ring with my father's initials? I took it off
    without thinking and let him weigh it in his hand.

THE NIGHT WE WERE DYLAN THOMAS

for Suzanne Cleary

In ways we were a most unlikely group: Mark engaged
and David with his thick mustache and beard, you
a sophomore and me in my first year, our friendship
sown in a farming town, upstate New York,
in stark-lit rooms and the Rathskeller where
one Friday afternoon we drank pitcher after pitcher
of beer and one by one composed a line and passed it on
until it grew … incomprehensible. More unlikely
was that summer's night on the Upper East Side
we converged to eat spaghetti. Was it David's
or Mark's idea to hop a cab to the Village,
the city singing, the driver speeding
to the heaving bar on Hudson? Was it you or Mark or David
who propped an elbow on the counter, looked up
to strike that pose? Then the rest of us in turn, unlikely
as it was even to be there, not that anyone seemed to notice
or care as we paused and waited, one by one, for someone
to click a camera and make us famous.

HERSHEY'S ICE CREAM PARLOR

Though all I wanted was a single scoop of chocolate
    I've ended up eating a hot fudge sundae

but who could resist? Here's a freezer full
    of peanut butter flavours, another of mint!

I'm in this strip mall by the library on the hottest day
    of the year, the hottest in years, I can hardly

breathe, and except for the high school girl
    behind the counter who could have been me

I'm the only person in this vast grey cavern,
    in a booth by the window, looking out on the parking lot

by the traffic lights and railroad tracks. American flags
    hang from the candy shop and pet supply,

the beauty shop where my mother has her hair done.
    The Fourth of July is just around the corner

with its annual parade, and rain, and for a moment
    I wonder what a grown woman like me is doing here

though the sundae is the best yet, the fudge hot,
    the whipped cream light and sweet. I even said yes

to the Red Dye Number 2 maraschino cherry, wanting
    the works. To go the full nine yards.

OYSTER BAY

The sun is still strong, searing our calves, scorching our thighs
as we walk down streets of elm trees knitted in stripes

and pinned with names on small white cards, past
the post office built in '36, its vaulted ceiling

Sistine Chapel-like, and the '50s restaurant
packed with deep red booths and deluxe burger platters.

Wanting to be someplace else we've driven here
to find architects' buildings in miniature, windows

the size of postage stamps, every door a jewel,
each wall and roof tile; and we discover the Townsend House,

built in 1740 and home to George Washington's spy
while Theodore Roosevelt pauses by the bandstand

on the green, and the ice cream shack on the corner
serves a perpetual stream of customers. In that space between

the edge of town and the beach, where who knows who
gets up to who knows what, we pass a parking lot

full of locked up vans, their windows baked and bleached.
Popcorn! Chicken Tasters! Cotton Candy! Psychic!

the signage screams. And of course there is a merry-go-round
and of course as we cross the railroad track – quick –

to catch sails on the horizon, a house nestled among evergreens,
the sun continues to pursue us, pressing, pressing,

while the Long Island Sound laps the pebbles, cools our toes.

STORMWATCH ON LONG ISLAND

My brother-in-law warns of forty-mile winds
    coming in from the west, the fiercest storm in decades,
        says he'll sit on the front step of the house
           to watch it roll in.

When a sheet of cloud steals over Jerusalem Avenue,
    the newly burst pink and white azaleas, the stretches
        of cherry blossoms along Holiday Park Drive,
           and when the red-leafed maples begin to nod

uncontrollably in the bluster, I suddenly want to be out there –
    so I hop in the car and drive past Seaford and continue
        east on Sunrise Highway past Massapequa,
           Massapequa Park, Amityville, Copague …

to the next town and the next to where the sky
    is not yet threatening, to where it's still full of light
        and I can chase it if I want, all the way to Montauk Point
           if I want, even as it grows darker and darker
                behind me.

THINGS WE'LL NEVER KNOW

At the candy shop on Lex after a morning
at the Met: we're trying to choose
between two eggs on toast and a two-egg sandwich,
both fried, neither coming with a side,
so what's the difference?

We claim a booth at the back
beyond the swivel stools at the counter;
it's a welcome den on a hot, hot day,
the sun doesn't miss a beat. Here
where there's hardly light

what air there is
is churned by a fan in the corner.
As for the waitress: grumpy by nature
or just tired? We ask about the difference
but it remains a secret, and it takes only a bite

to realize our mistake. Maybe the two eggs on toast
have runny yolks or thicker bread
slathered in butter. Maybe we should have
chosen something else, someplace better.
I pay at the register

covered in silver whirls
like the handles of guns in Westerns and wonder
about the collection of old Coca-Cola bottles,
row after row of them boiling in the window.

THE AMERICAN FOOT IN ENGLAND

It's time to say something about the American foot.
How difficult to fit – some subtle difference.
Hard to get the measure even nearly right – and then the price!
Enough of the French foot, the Italian and Spanish.
In New York shoes were a hobby.
I was voted best-shod woman on the third floor at Macmillan,
had a collection to rival Imelda Marcos's.

At a two-by-four shop on Lex and 59th so crowded you couldn't
flip a dime, I fell for pink ballet slippers, sandals the colour of yolk,
sunny green mules with small white daisies of leather.
But my biggest coup? A pair to match my wedding gown,
not ivory or oatmeal or bone, but the perfect confection of linen.
It was then I knew to buy shoes was to buy a piece of the city.

USES FOR A WEDDING DRESS

At first he thought she had lost her mind, then took out
    the dress on Saturdays and laid it on their bed, unzipped
the plastic sheath and stroked the satin tresses, rows of tiny buttons,
    thinking, *You can make someone happy but you can't*
make it last. Lord, he'd tried. And now he took the sharpened shears
    from the kitchen drawer and cut a square, like a window,

from the front of his ex-wife's wedding dress and dusted the bookcase,
    the piano and lampshades, then the places she couldn't reach.
When the car needed washing, he cut a piece from the bodice
    and sensed, inside, an easing, then used a sleeve
to clean his son's football boots, the other to wash
    the kitchen floor, the grimy fabric giving him

a certain satisfaction. He scrubbed the rings around the bath and sink,
    made a banner for his daughter's county match, bunting
for her birthday. Strips, like bandages, scared birds
    from his allotment, and with the final threads he flossed
his teeth and mended bed sheets. By the time he found the veil
    to strain spaghetti, he barely remembered her face.

NEBRASKA

Was it due to the size of the screen,
its angle on the back of the seat, or a twisted
transmission of pixels, a clever sleight of hand

but whose hand? All I know
is that when my glasses came off I could see
the pair of them, father and son, crossing

the plains of Nebraska, clouds overhead,
a town's white church and steeple.
Every one of the old man's wrinkles.

Screws in a hinge, miraculous
single bead of light on a lip,
speck on a tooth.

Thirty thousand feet above the sea
I think of the woman in Gateshead
who could hear for the first time at forty

and my mother back on Long Island
who fears she's lost a little bit more
of her vision each time I see her.

ON MY MOTHER NOT RESETTING HER WATCH

Whenever they came to England she'd live
on New York time, delighted at the thought

of staying five hours behind. We could be out
having lunch in Lewes or London and she'd glance

at her wrist. 'My watch says eight which means ...
it must be one!' My dad would forward his watch

as soon as the pilot gave word, and on landing
at Heathrow my parents would live in both times

at once, and in two places, thinking of home
but not daring to read a paper. Now, on her own,

my mother still won't succumb to being here
completely, asks about the value of the pound,

scrutinizes coins in her palm. She can fly home
and pretend she'd never left.

Thousands of miles apart, we speak
on the phone all the time, her days, my nights.

CHANCES ARE

When they ask if she would dance and then to what –
Sinatra? Dean Martin? – she tells them Johnny Mathis.
It has always been Johnny Mathis.

They take my mother's jeans, her watch and hearing aids
(I wear the watch, I watch the aids) and dance her down
the hounds-tooth carpet, through armoured doors:
No wrenches and trolleys, dolleys and pacemakers –
to join Johnny singing 'Chances Are', her favourite.

His voice would fill our house on Tuesday mornings
as she dusted-polished-vacuumed, as she washed and washed,
furious and determined, to his voice like caramel.
Sometimes Doris Day joined us with 'Pillow Talk'.

Now in a blue paper dress they have her lying down,
still as a doll, to the sounds of hammering and a drill's
pound, pound. 'I didn't expect this!' she cries
to the high-pitched *clicks* of rubber-bands stretching,
the tune of fingers snapping. *'Is it done yet?'*

'How ya doin', sweetheart?' the technician calls.
'Don't move for the next two minutes.' The pinball beep's
insistent. Through double doors I hear my mother groan,
resolving to keep her legs, her arms, from dancing.

A SKI DREAM IN WHICH NO ONE WAS SKIING

I was talking in a kitchen to someone about skiing
but I couldn't really ski – the last time I tried

I fractured my knee, filled my bones with bruises.
Now at the hotel I was heading towards the dining hall,

it was already packed, and on the other side
my parents were wearing the Burberry trench coats

they bought the year I studied in London, my mom looking
not like my mom in her matching Burberry hat.

They were queuing at a counter; I would reach them
before they saw me, but my sister approached

and asked if the leggings I wore were hers.
Was it my dad who spotted me first

or my mother? I knew only that as I got closer
the cat stretched and I pulled up the covers

and for the rest of the day willed myself back to the cold
and the crowd, back to my parents in their Burberry coats.

DINNER WITH THE TWO HOWARDS

I keep returning to the two Howards, to that night
they glanced up from their table for four
and gestured for us to join them
though they'd already ordered, how well spoken
and eager, even my mother was pleased, and surely by now
they must have known her by sight. One Howard
was an engineer at GE and still gave lectures there,
the Howard whose wife was having dinner
with friends of the woman whose husband died
just that day, we'd heard Kimberley at Reception –
It's a 999! – that kerfuffle in the hallway, so Howard
was having dinner with Howard, who, after he'd finished
his coffee and pie, began to excuse himself to catch
the BBC World Service. *The BBC– !* I blurted, as if
I'd been away longer, and for the next half hour Howard
revelled in stories of his Elderhouse visit to Caerphilly,
Betws-y-Coed, Cardiff Castle – *I was there last week!* –
and in the morning Emily, the first Howard's wife,
came over to introduce herself and thank us.

UPSTATE NEW YORK MAH-JONGG

It's not played as it's played on Long Island, at least
that's what my mother says, complaining,
or explaining, that the women play more slowly here,
their fingers less dexterous, hands less exciting, she's
incensed that the pot is fifty cents instead of seven dollars.
She didn't ask to spend time in this communal space
where anyone can come to knit or piece a puzzle together –
far better to meet at a neighbour's kitchen table with
an urn of coffee, platters of sandwiches and melon.
My mother yearns for her twice-weekly game – Tuesdays
at ten thirty, Wednesday nights – with like-minded friends
she's known for decades, can talk to, some much younger,
one the same age as me, tells us the women here lack
a certain … are not what she'd expected, so my sister invites
her own friends to come by for a morning of mah-jongg
at the independent living complex my mother calls
'the place' and I call 'the palace', where some are true
aficionados while others haven't begun to learn.

I THINK OF OLIVE

I think of Olive, who lived well
into her nineties and ended up in a care home
down the road from The Hare, in Speldhurst,

and I think of my mother in her new apartment
with its spick-and-span cream carpets
and a view of gardens from the terrace

and how Olive left her house on Ravenswood
kicking and screaming, I loved her for that,
satisfied to have nothing to do with anyone

while my mother left Wantagh brokenhearted
after more than sixty years, *Bye, house*
the only words that escaped as we pulled down the drive.

At first Olive refused to sit with the others at supper,
insisting on eating from a tray on her lap
while propped on the side of her bed, whereas

my mother goes down happily now
to the dining room where she's waited on,
or the bistro that serves brunch all day

on Wednesdays. It wrenched our hearts
when Olive joined the circle round a blaring TV,
twisting her hands, looking forward to the end

of our visits, while just this evening on the phone
my mother whispers: *Don't tell your sister,*
I want you to be the one to get me out of here.

SOMETHING LIKE THAT

… or maybe nothing like that: the siftings and sortings,
wrapping and unearthing – photos, letters, certificates, receipts
stretching back sixty years, so something like that
but faster, faster, more final.

And then to find someone – anyone – to remove
the piano she loved but never played, covered
with photographs, the piano that echoed my practicing
after school, Dad's show tunes. Of everything,

the breakfront of porcelain treasures, some her mother's,
some her grandmother's, it was the piano
that found her trembling in a corner of the den
when the men arrived with a van that took ages

to reverse up the drive, bring close
to the low brick wall at the edge of the lawn. Was it slow
motion or fast we watched as they rolled it down the hall
over her precious wooden floor and then to the door

to hesitate, take a deep breath before stepping over
and down to the steps and the sloping lawn? Was it
in sure hands? So easily it could have gone
sprawling on the grass, so readily

it could have given up and cracked –
strings and ivory, wood and lacquer
buried in the dark evening grass.
Instead it went into the van whose doors

shut with such a thud it echoed and echoed
as they drove down the street.

GETTING LOST AT THE BEACH

We're talking about our mother's house, where we
grew up, and my sister says she feels nothing now,
she can even think of our father
without any sense of loss, and our stepdad,
who saved us, and that when her children

would run to her after a fall, scraped elbow, trouble
at school, she'd cradle them on her knee
and say, 'Life's tough, you may as well get used to it.'

I tell her I never understood how, when
I was six or seven, and she maybe five,
we strayed from our parents' blanket at the beach,
got lost among the hundreds – probably thousands –
of parasols packed on the sand

and I was the sister who panicked, while she
took my hand and led the way, said
if she was the younger one why was I
the one crying. She found the lifeguard
and did the talking, and the lifeguard

lifted us up to a stand that towered in the heat
under a sky so blue it was painful, and we scoured
the scorching beach in search of a familiar pattern
not unlike every other pattern in that same forest green
and somehow found the one

in a million that sheltered our parents
in its shade, and it was she who had the courage
to run barefoot across that blistering sand.

MY MOTHER REVISITS LONG ISLAND

for Aimee and Warren Hirschhorn

… though not where she lived for sixty-
plus years but farther east, where it's flat
and green, ribboned with inlets, where the houses
stretch like endless sandy beaches, the horizon
so low – infinity is farther there.
And the air! Laced with salt, a hint
in every breath, it's always there, and at night
when a breeze comes off the sea there's
something so … so inexplicably
freeing there, she feels it there,
she's alive.

When we speak on the phone there's
a brightness in her voice, a lilt, a lift
I haven't heard for months, nearly
a year, and it makes me wonder
if it was ever there, or always there,
but here it is, as if the very air
has turned back years and years and suddenly
she is here again, and she
is young. *It was so lovely,* she says, as she
never says, *just sitting by the pool, just
talking – just being there.* I want to say
Hold on to that, don't let it get away, Mom,
don't let it go.

SPEAKING WITH MY MOTHER THROUGH A STORM

I time my call so that
there's time to have a swim
before we have to walk the dog
and think of dinner, but then the sky's
completely grey, a solid grey, a grey
like stone, like steel, the trees
are being whipped, the wind
is fierce, I fear my neighbour's tree will lift
and fly away, above the pavilion in the park,
into the wood. The thunder drumrolls,
then crashing rain.
Can you hear it? I ask
holding the phone to the window.
Thousands of miles
get in the way: my mother, on the deck
of her apartment in the blazing sun,
can't hear a thing.

THE SUN IS SHINING

as bright as the day I took the train
from the city to upstate New York and was again lifted
by the colours of the autumn leaves, revived
by the fire of vivid reds and yellows, so alive
in their dying, more than our autumns here in England.
All along the Hudson, the trees themselves and then
their mirror-image, and then again reflected
in the windows of the train without
diminishing. I caught the first departure
from Grand Central, only to be delayed
somewhere between Ossining and Albany, stopped dead
on the track. Then to begin – and to be stuck again.
I checked the time and checked the time, it became a tic,
kept texting my sister for updates, imagining
her waiting by the bedside. The woman sitting next to me
was visiting her mother too, she hadn't seen her in years,
she'd had to cobble together the fare for the ticket
from her neighbours. What were the chances we'd be
thrown together on that particular day in that carriage?
Of course we'd tell the stories of our lives
before eventually pulling into Schenectady and I
flew to the car park and into the car with whoever it was
was speeding to the hospital, then I raced through the
    doors and into a lift,
alighting in a room to find her …
still, the silence of her deep untroubled sleep.
Oh, Mother, it was all I could do
to stop myself from crawling in beside you.

VISITING THE SECOND FLOOR

I picture the bank of lifts and the lift, the heft
and shine of it, neat rows of numbers, the rising up,

picture the opening doors and sudden light, the carpet,
soft, underfoot, the quiet, then stepping out into a hallway

with its nurses' station, voices, tapping of keys, bleeping
of monitors, the sense of people in bed or propped on a chair

and then people in beds and on chairs. The slowness
of it all, the quiet that is not quiet, the sighing

and the sighs. The door is open, I can enter and
I do and she is here and I walk towards her,

still able to walk towards her, to be with her, here
with my mother she's still here.

MOTHER

From the height of her hospital bed, one hand
    reaching down, the other stretched out to us,

my mother said, *I'll miss you* as she hovered, longingly,
    between the plot of earth beside our father and baby brother

and here, with my sister and me, our faces couldn't be closer
    as we pleaded, knowing it wasn't fair

to want her back. *I'll miss the children's smiles*, she said
    and in that breath, *I'm sorry I can't take you out to dinner*,

my mother, who'd worn a tube in her nose and when it was enough
    they cut the blue of it and drew it out, inch by patient inch

down to the bloodied end, then slipped it in a bin,
    all done; who'd learned to walk again, one-two, one-

two, first with her shiny new hip, then with smooth shiny legs
    she could be proud of after first being bundled and hoisted

till her feet touched ground and at last she could begin to stand
    alone again. Mother, even living in the suburbs, fear

held a knife under your pillow when we were little, my mother
    when I was sick and crying, desperate

to shut out the world, you held me and conjured
    buttered toast so perfect I believed you'd invented it.

STARLING

Starling Day Gewent (b. 2019)

Every morning my mother asks, *Is she here yet?*
which breaks our hearts a little more, and then it's

Lazy baby! her voice tinged with humour, tinged
with anger, it's hard to tell. Another time my mother says

The baby's been born, hasn't she? knowing we know
that once the baby's here, our mother

can slip away. And then that time she accuses us
of lying. Oh, Mother, we could never lie to you.

The news arrives, the cries, relief –
and for a while my mother

talks about the family wedding – she has to buy
a dress! – and how she'll stock the fridge

with grapes, her favourite cheese – then suddenly
she's asleep. For days no one can rouse her

till one morning she stirs from her ocean depths
and, with whatever energy can possibly be left

in her withered arms, she holds that baby, looks at her
as if into a distant sky, whispers her name.

BLACK CLOTHES

And that night I took off the black
corduroy skirt I'd bought at M&S
days earlier, not wanting to borrow one

from my sister, pulled off the black
scooped-neck top that always
makes me feel better, its snug fit,

clean lines. Peeled off the black tights,
unzipped the boots that rose mid-calf,
that stood me well in winter with their

thick stitches, strong soles. Off, cashmere
sweater, your fine jet buttons, and the scarf
from Suzanne, brightest turquoise,

defiant. What next? The day gotten through,
over, I could go to bed and not sleep,
maybe not ever, not like I used to.

RED LENTIL SOUP WITH LEMON

I want to tell you
about the soup I made, red lentil
with lemon, which is what Anita prepared –
prepared being your word –
in the days that followed your funeral
when she invited the cousins for lunch
on the Upper West Side.
It was unseasonably warm, Gil
was there too and they'd be off travelling
again next year, which is this year, which is this
pandemic year. I couldn't have come over
to visit you, but our nightly phone calls
would have kept us going,
they kept me going – and your love

of detail! What I had
for dinner or who said what
at work, all my little 'nonsenses'
as you called them, as I brought my world
closer to yours growing smaller,
powder blue bathrobe, TV in Terri's old room.
I could tell you all the essentials
and inconsequentials as if we were together
at your kitchen table, the minutes and minutiae
of our lives, the things that count most:
the lentil and carrot of it, the onion and garlic,
the gloriously ordinary,
each day for me, morning for you.

EGG SALAD

Always my grandmother's recipe: cover the eggs
   and boil for thirteen minutes, leave to cool till morning,
so when I crack the shells against the yellow saucepan
   Jeanne left when she returned to New York they shatter

like glass, like the windscreen Mr Cooper took a hammer to,
   the segments glittering and intricate, perfect
for the stained-glass windows we made in his art class
   senior year at Wantagh High, mine a purple magnolia

my parents hung in the window overlooking the deck.
   I remove the shells and return the eggs to the water,
ensure they are smooth all over, and with the slicer
   my Aunt Etta bought in the dollar store on my visit to Holiday,

Florida – her disbelief I didn't already own one, my young son's
   fascination – I slice first one way, then the other
to form small squares of egg, like mosaics, like teeth,
   then into the wooden chopping bowl, uneven and worn,

rescued from the charity box after we cleared out
   my mother's apartment, the beautiful one she grew
to hate. Debbie said to leave it, I'd be better off
   with something new and hygienic, but as I add mayonnaise

and mix I feel relieved, and glad, that I couldn't let go
   of my mother's hands as they held the wooden-handled chopper
or the sound of it against the bowl as she made the best egg salad,
   chicken salad, chopped liver – she did, my mother, this bowl.

VISITATIONS

Every night, often between three and four, sometimes earlier –
at one or two – I meet my mother

on the deck of her Long Island home, or sometimes in the kitchen
with its vase of carnations and often a visiting niece,

nephew, grandchild, sometimes a neighbour – she had such
good neighbours – or we're at the beach,

the place she loved best, even when she could walk
only as far as the boardwalk, sit on a bench and watch the sea,

the sea. Due to her love of shopping
sometimes we meet in one of those endless

luxury parking lots, drive from one store
to the next, and once we met in a bingo hall – my mother sold

scratch-offs and cards filled with numbers, those fat
tubes of ink with the sponge at the end while someone called

29, rise and shine! 85, staying alive! 22, toot, toot! We've explored
the caves at Lascaux, though neither of us had ever been

or mentioned them, and just last night I was pounding a door
crying, *Let me see my mother.*

THE YOGURT POT

Taking from under the sink
the small square
bucket of peelings and cores,
of wilted leaves,
then crossing the garden –

I realised that you'd never
seen this simple act before:
me taking off the lid
of the compost bin
and tipping in
what we couldn't use, return it

to the earth
of bedding plants
and rows of lettuce and radish,
cabbage and rainbow kale
we eventually grew.
How little you really knew
of my life here.

And by the apple tree
a memory
of the summer
we cleaned out your fridge
and found a pot of yogurt, orange
with mould, so much of it

I didn't have
the patience to scrape it clean,
rinse it under the tap and add
the gleaming pot

to the upright paper bag
you kept in the closet by the door.

You found it in the bin
and did what I hadn't time
or energy for, not even the
presence of mind
to hide it from you.

You stood at that sink
and washed out that yogurt pot
so matter-of-factly,
not saying a word.

THE FAINTING GAME

Back in the days of sleepovers
(we must have been twelve or thirteen,
there were fifteen of us at least)
we'd gather in someone's basement
with its wood panelled walls
and hi-fi system, maybe
a sliding bar. It was
always someone's birthday

and at some point in the evening
we'd take it in turns:
one of us would stand behind another
and hold her under the arms
while she took deep
long breaths, again
and again, till she became lightheaded,
held her final breath
and leaned back
to be lifted

off her feet,
her legs going limp, all of her
limp, turned to jelly, then
to lower her gently,
you had to be gentle,
see her crumple.
Wait.
She'd be out cold
for what seemed like ages

before opening her eyes,
surprised
to have been
somewhere else entirely,
then to come back.
They always came back.

SCENES OF THE OLIVE

I

At first you can't see them
for their colour, the same lazy
grey-green leaves they hide between,
droplets on a stem like a thread.
Identical neat
spears of leaves, the gentle bones
of fish, their shadow in sunlight.
It is evening.
The sky is offering its brightness still.

II

In the neighbouring field, someone's
deserted the white walls of a house,
its row of aqua tiles left
glinting and winking in the heat.

We head for the interior.
A totem pole of signs
jostles for attention: Sandra's Bar,
free bananas, Saki's apartments.
Zakinthos 5.
Pottery Studios this way.

III

It is even hotter
when I see a man
perched on a chair
under a tree, his feet
submerged in water,
the plastic tub round
and green.

IV

Their craggy bark reminds me
of honeycomb, it symmetry
of darkness. And then old skin,
crusty limbs, all elbows
and hollows.
The ground is parched, waiting
and waiting for rain.

V

In the town that was not destroyed
by earthquakes
curtains hang in windows,
tables and chairs stand outside front doors.
The road is hard dust.
In a circle of grass, brittle as bone,
the olive carries its fruit
these two thousand years.

TSILIVI BEACH

This is how it happens: a crescent of beach
swarming with people, and then an innocent sea.

In the distance, a line of buoys strung between
two headlands, the swimmers no more than specks

against mountains of neighbouring islands.
The water is calm. I am sitting on my towel

with its pattern of fish, my bag overflowing with
bottles of water, lotions, brochures of boat tours,

fearing that two of those swimmers out there now
are my daughters, their heads dark and slick and bobbing,

their strong legs kicking as if nothing could happen,
as if speedboats never enter these waters

meant for swimmers only, not meaning to, not
meaning anything as waves grow higher and whiter,

the swimmers mistaken for something else entirely.

ARRIVING IN FISKARDO

We arrived in the dark
and the lapping of water.

At five I woke
to the crescent moon,
the hunter never closer

his belt never brighter,
and this body of water,
this stillness of mountain,

the landscape in focus:
lights in two houses
like candles, a whisper.

FOKI BEACH

The masts of the boats reaching straight to the sky
are perfect and the boats themselves, all sleek
on the water in the harbour

and each of the rocks lining the bay
and the mountains behind, and those behind them,
paler, more reaching, more out of reach.

As for the sky, its blue, blue, blue
is a perfect pitch between here and there
and the clouds that adorn it with expert brushstrokes.

And the water itself, what could be more
perfect than the colour of some semi-precious stone,
a green-blue/blue-green you thought

you could only imagine, then the glass
clearness of the water. And the rocks below
covered in coral or algae where tiny silver-green

fish dart and weave. As for the temperature,
you who never swim waded in knee-deep,
thigh high and swam like you'd not done since

you were a child, I didn't know you could swim,
and then you lay on your back
and let the water carry you.

'This could heal us,' I said. When the shadows
stretched across the bay and approached
the white pebble beach, even they were perfect.

LETTER TO MY CHILDREN FROM THE BEACH

The last time I saw your father in the water
was when you were young
and he stood in the shallow end of the pool
on a campsite in Cheddar, held out his arms
as each of you kicked and stretched and reached,
maybe swallowed some water as the sun played
on your foreheads and you propelled yourselves,
smiling and proud, relieved and nearly exhausted
till he cradled you. And there was a time
before you were born when he and I swam
among Roman columns as small blue spears of fish
darted between our feet.

Right now while I'm on the shore at Kimilia
he's lying on his back in the water,
kicking in slow motion – nothing
could be better – then turns and smiles as if
he's having the time of his life, as if
he's living the life he'd imagined.

THE GREEN HOUSE

I like everything about the small green house:
its orange roof-tiles that stretch
over the porch, its neat white fence,
the steps that lead up from the road. I like
the road's bend and how the house is positioned
just so, above it, in the middle, where
occasionally a car or coach or motorbike
passes by. From here, one large window, curtains
behind the dark green screen, and beside it
the proud white square of the air conditioning.
Are they lavish baskets or next door's bougainvillea
that fill the porch? And what about
the other houses? I watch and watch
but no one enters or leaves.

ASYLUM

I would gather all of them
who roam these roads
and wait under cars
and huddle in doorways, on stairs,
who lie on windowsills and steal out
whenever someone passes
in the hope of food. I would de-flea
each and every one, and give them
little beds to sleep in. I would name them:
Glister, Mimi, Geronimo, Zeus, and serve up
dishes of cream as a special treat.
And they would fill each corner and crevice
of my abundant house, they could
have it all. And I would stroke
their narrow heads, tickle their fine thin ears,
make sure they ate well
and had some privacy and a chance
to lie in the shade if they wanted.

SILVER SCREEN

Among the mountains and the stars, the water's gentle tapping,
  two luminous moons appear – maybe Bogart and Bergman,
   maybe Rogers and Astaire – above the Ionian Sea.

The ship arrived at dusk with masts devoid of sails, smaller
  than a liner and not the usual white, nor was it
   floodlit but grew darker in the dark, its deck

full of figures we couldn't hear or see from our balcony
  as we finished our meal. How sudden the change in view
   from placid sea to something almost military, ludicrous

as a shark in the quiet of the harbour. We stood in a hush
  of olives, it was towards the end of our stay and the island
   was folding its umbrellas, shops were shutting

for the season and soon we'd be asleep under our canopy
  while out there, for all the world to witness, was a couple
   declaring what could only be their love.

HOTEL PALARINE

for Marissa

When we're not back till nine one night she embraces us
and leads us to dinner, Rosalina from Argentina,
who hears my accent and tells us she loves New York, who
used to visit every year, sometimes twice a year, and at nineteen
looked after a boy in a town outside Darien. Now he's twenty-six,
lives on Twenty-something Street and she can stay there.
She wants to live in New York City, but she's with Jorge.
She loves Jorge but Jorge loves living in Andorra
despite what he has to do: magic at the hotel pub, all those close-up
table tricks, pretend to be one of the Three Kings
on Epiphany, when every town has a parade and the children
dressed as pirates throw sweets from elaborate floats.
Jorge knew someone who knew someone
who got Rosalina a job taking the drinks orders at dinner
and setting out trays of croissants for breakfast
though she doesn't like it, never mind having only one day off
each week. She has saved a two-for-one voucher for the spa
at Calisa for when her sister visits. Rosalina and Jorge have been here
two months. She's a qualified accountant, kept her feet
beneath a desk for seventeen years and answered to no one.
She doesn't miss it. Yes, of course she's on email.
And *Sí, sí, sí*, on Facebook too.

PARIS

for Eva

I said goodbye to the river and the cafés, the shutters and the tall
blue doors, the wrought-iron railings, the balconies and flowers,
roads slick with rain, the rain. I said goodbye to umbrellas,
to people walking on the streets, pushchairs
and jewellery shops, clothing shops and boutiques
full of brightly patterned scarves, to the scarves. I said goodbye
to the rainbow-coloured balloons, to celebrations
on Saturday night, to small dogs on the ends of leads, boulangeries,
windows full of cheese, to the students
next to us at that restaurant where we sat in a corner
at the back, specialities written on a blackboard, one cold bottle of wine.
I said goodbye to my daughter's studio apartment
and the courtyard lined with pots and all that green, the large brass
    lantern
suspended in the corner, to views from windows, to the night,
the air, to trees on rooftop patios. I said goodbye
to my daughter at the station, watched her walk away in her raincoat,
caught one last glimpse of her raincoat.

MY DAUGHTER TURNS INTO A FISH

for Eva

We swim the lengths in harmonious turquoise strokes,
    as if to smooth out the years

we've not done this together, or since my daughter
    has touched water, now that she no longer

competes in galas. No thought of overtaking
    or racing, we don't bother to count laps

or create waves but glide with ease as we chat
    side by side, like other women.

I want to keep things slow
    because they matter. I want to hear every word

my daughter has to utter and for us to stretch this day
    until we can stretch it no farther, a privilege

to have this time together. When we feel ready
    we will enter the steam room, sauna, Jacuzzi,

and eventually the woman at the desk will beckon us
    for our treatments. How can there be

this joy now and more later? On what turns out
    to be her final length, my daughter

dives down and deep along the bottom, suddenly
    sprouts gills and fins and tail, a rare

new breed. She swims and swims
    effortlessly, until she's no longer my daughter.

LITHE / ALIVE

for Susan Wicks

Sometimes I lie awake at night, muscle-tired,
bone-tired, after another Sunday afternoon
swim with Sue, after the walk
from her house to the pool, each of us
telling the other her news
against the backdrop of St John's traffic

before we slip into the blue – baby blue,
no, turquoise, the turquoise of the earrings
my father bought me one summer
from the side of a road in New Mexico.
'I saw them and thought of you,' he said.
In high school then, I wear them still.

Water on my skin, these lengths
the most important thing: nine of crawl
and every tenth of breaststroke, counting
and repeating, swimming
for my life.
            Our neighbour's husband drowned
on some beach at the end of Long Island.
Those lakes in upstate New York were so cold
they could stop your heart.
                        After twenty,
something lightens and lifts, almost ceases
to exist, I can breathe again. To be underwater
and then to snatch some air, legs
well oiled, arms reaching out for ever.

SLIVER

Swimming in the evening before dinner, wasps
busy under the eaves, the sun glowing orange, a sudden
snap in the September air as I lifted my arm from the water.
Maybe a nip of frost but it felt like a sliver
embedding in my thumb and pointer finger.

Counting lengths, without a thought of stopping,
I tried to ignore it, then willed it away
as it grew colder and was cold by the time I dragged myself
shivering from the water. Whatever it was remained
in the night – nights there were silver – and all next day

and through winter. I've tried to keep it at bay
but it continues to be a reminder
of that week, that day, plums
dripping in the orchard, in the greenhouse
those dark clusters of grapes.

RETURNING TO BEACH HUT

'Scholars have recently learned that
Walt Whitman hardly ever left his room.'

The room welcomes you – sun-filled
    as you enter the ordered pale blue:
towels jelly-rolled on the bed, more
    cupboards than you'll use, the right size alcove

to work in. A window full of waves,
    a red ship riding the horizon that makes you
believe there's some inherent good
    in returning, not even changing

the view. Something unfinished
    has brought you here to watch couples stroll
along the seawall before dinner,
    children run in sunken gardens – even this row

of garage doors and the redbrick wall
    where sparrows briefly perch. You look out
on grass verges and telephone wires,
    the day a steady grey and seagulls calling.

KITCHEN WINDOW, WELLS-NEXT-THE-SEA

The window of the second kitchen
in what was once a railway house
    looks out on salt-flecked

stones hauled from the sea
and a latticed fence
    where sweetpeas climbed

in summer, now flakes of paper
by a single frozen rose.
    Through the middle pane

another window
where a woman wearing an apron
    leans over

a sink of bubbles,
below the clock above the cupboard,
    her pearl earring framed

by a wave of wavy hair
as she leans and dips
    while from somewhere

out of this grey afternoon the sun
alights on the casement
    and a gold leaf rises. Light hovers

then brightens, follows her
as she enters another room,
    then another.

THE LIGHTHOUSE KEEPER

She used to stop right there, where the cliffs jut
    and the gorse is scented vanilla, where

chaffinches feed and dart. From the lighthouse
    I would watch her gaze at Devil's Throat

which once ate villages whole, then spat them out.
    Some say they hear the bells of Shipdean Church

still singing underwater. I used to see her
    walk alone, then later saw her with someone

and then again as they picnicked with their children
    against the backdrop of fishermen's cottages

and a pier that spidered the horizon.
    We'd pan the sea, each in our way, never

exchanging a word, until I left the white-housed
    beacon for good, the sound of the sea still

stinging my ears. And she? That's her bench,
    something about love, about memory.

TWELVE OF US

for friends at the Kent & Sussex Poetry Society

One of us drinks espresso in Nelson's
at a table puckered in seersucker,
sun breaking through glass doors

as one of us saunters past with hands in pockets,
legs bouncing in jeans, diagonally, to the shops

while one down at the harbour
eats Dutch pancakes on *The Albatros*:
fresh blueberries with cream and a cup of tea.

One of us sits on a bench along the quay
sketching boats as the tide stretches out

and two of us are back from the beach already,
her scarf of ribbon, the camera round his neck,

while another is out by the beach huts
where children are tossing Frisbees
and dipping their feet in the sea.

Three of us are driving to get here,
one more is boarding a train

while one of us is anywhere – back at the house
or walking through pine forests, marshlands,
maybe nearing Cromer, maybe further.

CRAB POTS

They once had a purpose, are now
    washed up like rubbish,
yellow ropes and aquamarine, faded
    and unravelling through broken rims;
        one is crushed like a can.

Someone would have risen before dawn
    to lay down the bait
in the chambers, lay the pots
    along the sea's long shank and mark them
        with a buoy and flag. A day's work,

a life's work, the sea beckoning and roiling,
    the wind's sharp slap. In the end
nothing but to count the catch, weigh up
    what to keep for the table
        and how much to sell.

No one will reclaim them now,
    even know they are here. The tide is a rush
and one is overturned like a turtle,
    its underside's music of metal
        a rich brown rust.

MARSH MALLOW

February cold blowing in from the sea and like everyone else
I brace against the wind, shivering, then enter
Jagger chemist on Staithe Street, sneezing and filling tissue
after tissue. The pharmacist appears from behind the divide
as my eyes start streaming, nods as if he knows, his eyes
drooping slightly in that understanding way as he explains
that I need something gentle (he says this gently) and hands me
a bottle of syrup made from the root of the mallow which grows
in the marshes, maybe even here, and a pack of mallow lozenges.

What do I know of marshmallows but those pink and white pillows
of sugar I ate at funfairs when I was little that later
made me sick, or the miniature ones my mother dotted
on top of hot chocolate my sister and I drank with friends
after sledding, huddled in the garage. The pharmacist explains
that mallow is a herb and when I Google it later I learn
of its thick fleshy stem and five-petal flower, that the ancient
Egyptians boiled the root pulp with honey till it thickened,
strained it to soothe sore throats and coughs, heal wounds.
That it was only for those with royal blood, and gods.

IT'S A MARVELLOUS DAY FOR AN ENDOSCOPY

See? The sun is high, it's early – trucks
on the road, buses flying.
We could go to the beach! The city!

Instead we drive across town
to the hospital, the hospital,
for an early morning endoscopy.

The surgeon has a list as long
as my arm but I'm first in the queue.
'You're lucky,' he says,

'you get the clean 'scope!
I can't say that to everyone.'
In a gown open at the back, dotted

with diamonds, Japanese-like,
I'm reading Keats: *This living hand,*
now warm and capable …

when the nurse comes in
to puncture the back of my own hand,
ease in the catheter while my husband

holds my earrings in his pocket,
and my watch, our hands clasped
until I'm through to the other side.

ANAESTHESIA

Slowly I sank
as the anaesthetist was reminiscing
about the waves at Jones Beach
where he life-guarded weekends
those summers in the '70s
when he worked at a camp
in Westchester – maybe I knew it?

I'm surfing now, rising
from my stupor, coming up
for air, there's a figure hovering.
It's a peaceful fatigue as I'm wheeled
to my room and the nurse
takes my pulse and blood pressure,
        the numbers settling: 111, 110, 109 …
and again, right on time, I go under.

MEASURING

I measure my life in doses of heparin, in the syringes
    I plunge into my middle each night, and

in the daily washing of support socks, toe-less,
    bright-white; in leg-lifts and stretches, every step

I force myself to walk. I clock up each phone call
    and text, each email to colleagues, the ready-made

dinners my husband buys from Tesco, the time they take
    to heat while I struggle to set the table. See

how the days grow in increments as they tick, tick, tick
    till the next appointment with my consultant / physio-

therapist / psychotherapist, all the impossible stairs, each
    tab of codeine I drop into my mouth before sleep.

AFTER THE OP

from a table at Eat 17 with Jonathan and Emily

A couple chooses sandwiches
from behind glass doors.
He's wearing blue, she, grey and coral,
their colours a muted sunset,
and I can't help but notice how she shifts
from her right leg to her left, straightening

each knee, the smooth flex
of her limbs, and think, that's how
to do it, marvelling at the his-and-hers
of their deftness as they close the door
and stroll down the aisle, overcoming
each obstacle, every

impossible move. Through the window
I watch a woman walk with crutches,
a man with a stick. Whole families pass by.
A little boy, no older than two, walks
without effort. As for that girl running –
her feet barely touch the ground.

A DREAM OF WALKING

Sometimes, just before sleep,
I glimpse how it would feel
to walk again – the heaviness lifted, my
feet hovering over the floor,
a smoothness to my step.

One night I wake to the words:
A missing leg; a second language

and just last week my mother, at 94,
was given a new hip. In rehab she walks
with a Zimmer, soon she'll be doing stairs
and in a dream she is sprinting down a hill
in Central Park, past the carousel and zoo,

the bandstand and boating house,
Strawberry Fields forever.

THE KNEE DOES AQUAFIT

As if it wasn't enough of a feat
to arrive in one piece, but then to have to
navigate the changing room's
slippery tiles and puddles, that streak of silver
drain down the middle. I prop my sticks and hobble
to the showers, then, as if walking on glass, pick
my way to the water.
            All is blue crystal
as light strokes the surface, the music blaring,
the class in position and Paula singing
Babylove, oh, Babylove as a guard escorts me
to the edge, then takes away my crutches.
            How to describe
the texture of water, or honour the cool
as it holds me wholehearted.
Takes the weight of me, every last ounce of me,
without doubting or trying.

THE KNEE RIDES A BICYCLE

After giving itself a good talking to, the knee
takes itself in hand and hops on a bicycle.
It has been a long time and at first it fears
a stone might catch on a spoke and send it flying,
leave it sprawled on the path that on either side
is flanked by fields of new green grass
and overtakes, in the distance, a ribbon of stream
under a slender wooden bridge. O birdsong!
Bleating of sheep! The feel of the air and the smell
of wild garlic! Today the sun is generous,
the knee feels more assured with every tree it passes,
rhythm of pedals, turn of wheels, and how natural
now to say hello to other cyclists, their children
tucked in child-seats, dogs running along,
everyone smiling, the miles behind.

THE KNEE FLIES TO NEW YORK

Though the knee loves a window seat as much as
the next knee, as much as anyone, it chooses a seat
in the aisle, there's space to stretch out in, and always
a seat that is over a wing, supposedly the safest place
to be when you're thirty thousand feet in the air

with nothing but clouds, but sea. Buckled in, it watches
the cabin crew's pantomime about what to do
in an emergency, but even a knee knows in its heart…
It's not as naïve as other knees, had once come
unhinged – so unstable it fell in the road

as a car was passing. That cry for help, then
to be laid up completely dependent, demeaned,
as unprofessional as a knee
can't afford to be. It has ordered the vegan option
and a glass of red. On some flights the knee

is so tired it falls asleep while the plane is still
on the runway, sometimes soon after take-off, careful
to position itself so that no one will lean on /
walk into it on their way to the loo, trolleys
won't roll it down or swallow it in their wheels

but for now it does a sun salutation in the aisle
to recalibrate muscle and ligament, take stock
in this limbo, and neither dwell on what lies ahead
nor look for a sign, any sign, beyond a sky
full of emptiness and the wing's blinking eye.

THE HAPPINESS

for JWC

Stars shone that first night, a hint of red
in the air. I left my jacket in the office
and walked along Embankment past the Eye
to Waterloo. On the train it was
standing room only, and when I checked my phone
the message was there. Oh, I may have seemed
like everyone else: holding a pole, steadying
my legs, keeping that deadpan
expression on my face, but inside I was dancing

a mazurka and screaming at the top of my lungs.
And later as I walked up Silverdale, an inner –
a calm – *Was it real?*

*

How lithe my cat as she slips
out the front, enters the night, returns
through the back to curl like a shell, to curl
like a shell on a cushion. To reward
her long years, the soft vibration
in her throat, to indulge
her suppleness, I pour stars
in my palm, cream
in her dish, she stretches across my lap
as we watch a film about chocolate
but not *Chocolat*. I speak long distance
to my mother, of her neighbours'
trip to Splitz, how she's watering their plants.

*

The shock of my study: piles of paper, books,
laundry to put away, clothes to donate, recycle
in the bin by the gym. Wrapping paper, bubble wrap,
unread news or news to read again. The jaw of a deer,
its teeth intact, a shelf of shells and ragged fossils,
hardly a surface, a basket of postcards, photographs
in bulging carrier bags, every letter I've ever received,
pens, pencils, rubbers, envelopes, sticky notes
on envelopes, scraps. Sometimes
I teeter on despair, sometimes I think about
striking a match. Watch my life
go up in smoke. And then the knowledge:
I can still have the happiness despite all this.

*

Not to take for granted, to stay in bed
and drink a pot of tea from a china cup, then
take the dogs for a walk as a breeze stirs
the fur on their backs, as they rush into fields
of sunlight. And then, because it's the weekend,
we visit Basing House, where Henry VIII used to stay,
where children run on the lawn, disappear
into a tree while someone sketches the lake,
and where the coffee is second only
to the Black Dog's. We visit my sister-in-law
who lives near here, then traffic
on the M23, M25, A21,
those numbers home. All the while the fluttering
alive, flapping its wings and singing.

*

The hottest day of the year, the hottest September
on record. Someone is juicing apples – that smell
in the air – and there's washing everywhere, drying
in minutes. As if summer is beginning all over,
as if there will be more
dinners on the patio, sandals, heat
at the back of your neck.
A vase of fully opened roses. Sleeping
with windows wide, believing it can last.

*

The moon is full, what could be more?
It lights the sky, trees, grass,
these roofs and pavements. So visibly visible.
I want to look and look, not
miss a thing, miss out, this moment,
these moments. *Here I am, I am.*
I consider sleeping in the garden,
where we can be each other's reflection.

*

A week, a cause for celebration!
A toast at least. I make the Portuguese stew
with tomatoes ripe from the garden, infused with –
And I have loved every minute, even
the broken nights, was reminded of how
it felt to walk to Foki Beach from our apartment
in Greece, a cotton tunic sticking to my back, the heartbeat
of heat. Sitting on the train,
doing a hundred and one mundane –
Before it leaves
I will bury it deep enough to save.

SOMETIMES

Not occasionally or once in a while
but not as often as often, sometimes

everything is sometimes:
yogurt or cereal, coffee or tea,

working/not working. Sometimes
country, sometimes city. Sometimes

those vague washed-outs in between.
Swimming at the pool: sometimes

at night in the dark, sometimes
the sun streaming on shoulders,

loving it on shoulders. Sometimes
crowded and sometimes

all mine. Sometimes avoids
the absolutes; bolt-hole, escape

hatch, an out from the get-go.
The apple tree in flower

or full of tight green fruit.
The hangings on or lettings go

to rot on the ground. Apple juice,
sometimes jam, pie, compote, crumble.

MOON RIVER

It was Margaret who introduced us to The Woodman*
	that Saturday night. *A dying breed,* she said, *a step
back in time* – and maybe even more for us
	Americans. Through smoke and the notes

of a piano, in a room of red-flocked wallpaper, the laughter
	was husky, there was standing room only, and
when someone slipped through the door with a basket
	of cockles, she bought some. Above the din, the crowd

sang show tunes we didn't know, and when the mic
	was offered round, an American who lived in the other
wing of our hall strode up as if she'd done this before.
	In those high leather boots she'd worn all winter

while the rest of us fought being homesick, she clasped
	her hands, gazed ahead, and in a crystal-clear voice
we'd never heard, belted out a song about a river
	and the moon before the crowd joined in.

* Lee High Road, London, now Berhams Plumbing Supplies

CANARY-SHOULDERED THORN

for Caroline and Clive

Moths fly into our bathroom and hover,
     splay unremarkable wings against the tiles:
pencil shaving, edges
        of ragged paper. Woodchip beige,
    they seem the same but here

among the plum trees and the pears,
    yellow underwings appear, dappled carpets,
        common marbled and green, garden
      and spruce carpets; a shuttle-shaped dart, then
lured by the over-bright light they disappear

    down the slopes of the moth trap.
By chance I saw the one
    that hid in the lid of an egg box,
      which seemed neither insect nor moth

      but a bird
   so miniature it could fit
     on the end of a pen, its puff of yellow
  so like feathers, those wings.
And then that beak! Its eyes were beads.

    When you went to set it free
it perched on your finger,
    and as it flew into the night
      I could almost hear it sing.

HERON

for Martin

As if the afternoon had centred round its circling –
   its pterodactyl wings from out of nowhere
      reeling in the sky, our naked eyes following

as it homed in on the island. Numb with cold
   your fingers made adjustments to the telescope
      with such tenderness – that scar

on your thumb, these ridges of knuckle. The heron wore
   a shawl, in tatters, the fringe like the ends
      of a talis, tail feathers dragging. We saw it all

through the lens, a sadness, like mourning,
   while the heron stood against the wind,
      basked in the sun. All around us great tits dipped

and called *Teacher! Teacher!* as we talked
   of heading home, then heading home.
      I couldn't stop watching for some sign

or movement. The car was freezing,
   the afternoon already overripe
      and now this waiting and delaying

moving on, as if it mattered who left first
   or if the heron left at all,
      gathering its majestic weight to fly.

AUTHOR'S ACKNOWLEDGMENTS

I would like to thank the editors of the following publications in which some of these poems first appeared: *Iota, Magma, Poetry Ireland Review, Poetry News, Stand, The North, The Rialto* and *Under the Radar*.

'Canary-shouldered Thorn' was commended in the Gingko Awards 2018 and 'Hitch-hiking on Wantagh Parkway' was placed second in the Laureate's Prize 2018 (Poetry Business). 'In the Beginning' was short-listed for the Plough Poetry Competition 2019. 'Egg Salad' was long-listed in the 2020 National Poetry Competition.

With special thanks to my poet friends and first readers, especially Susan Wicks, Caroline Price, Mary Gurr and Suzanne Cleary, and to Tony Ward and Angela Jarman at Arc.

And with love and thanks to my family, as ever.

MARA BERGMAN grew up in Wantagh, New York, and graduated from the State University of New York at Oneonta. During her third year, she studied at Goldsmiths College and later made her home in the UK.

Mara's poetry has been published widely here and abroad. Her collection *The Tailor's Three Sons and Other New York Poems* won the *Mslexia* Poetry Pamphlet Competition and was published by Seren in 2015. In 2016, *Crossing Into Tamil Nadu* won a Templar Quarterly Pamphlet Competition. Her poems have been awarded prizes in the Troubadour competition and the Kent & Sussex Open Competition, among others. Her first full-length poetry collection, *The Disappearing Room*, was published by Arc Publications in 2018.

Mara works in London as an editor and is also an award-winning author of more than twenty books for young children. She lives with her husband in Tunbridge Wells and has three grown-up children.

www.marabergman.com